DATE DUE

			.

16.95

PREHISTORIC ART

Susie Hodge

Heinemann Interactive Library

Published by Heinemann Interactive Library
an imprint of Reed Educational & Professional Publishing,
1350 East Touhy Avenue, Suite 240 West,
Des Plaines, IL 60018

Designed by Plum Creative
Illustrations by Oxford Illustrators
Printed in Hong Kong / China

02 01 00 99
10 9 8 7 6 5 4 3 2

Library of Congress Cataloging-in-Publication Data
Hodge, Susie, 1960–
    Prehistoric art / Susie Hodge.
       p.   cm. -- (Art in history)
    Includes bibliographical references and index.
    Summary: Examines the art of prehistoric times, including painting, reliefs, sculpture, and pottery that has been found in Africa, the Pacific, and the Americas.
    ISBN 1-57572-553-3 (lib. bdg.)
    1. Art. Prehistoric--Juvenile literature.   [1. Art, Prehistoric.]
I. Title.   II. Series: Hodge, Susie, 1960–   Art in history.
N5310.H64   1997
709'.01--dc21   97–20677
                                                              CIP
                                                               AC

Acknowledgments
The author and publisher are grateful to the following for permission to reproduce copyright photographs:
cover photo: Colorphoto Hinz Allswil-Basel; all other illustrations: Ancient Art & Architecture Collection, M. Andrews p.29 (right), R. Sheridan pp.12, 14, 16, 17, 20, 22; Count Robert Bégoüen, Musée Pujol, Paris p.29 (left); The Bridgeman Art Library p.15; Colorphoto Hinz Allschwil-Basel pp.6, 10, 13; Corbis, W. Kaehler p.21, A. Woolfitt p.5; C. M. Dixon pp.7, 8, 19; Fortean Picture Library, D. Stacy p.28; Lauros Giraudon, Paris p.18; Robert Harding Picture Library, F. Jackson p.24, Larsen-Collinge Int. p.4; Werner Forman Archive, Anthropology Museum, Veracruz University, Jalapa p.26, Auckland Institute & Museum, Auckland p.23, British Museum p.25, Field Museum of Natural History, Chicago p.27

Our thanks to Paul Flux and Jane Shuter for their comments in the preparation of this book.

Every effort to contact copyright holders of any material reproduced in this book. Any omissions will be rectified in subsequent printings if notice is given to the publisher.

Cover picture:
Painted Bulls, Lascaux in France, about 12,000 B.C., Paleolithic, length of main bull is 18 ft, cave painting.

The most famous prehistoric art comes from the caves of hunters in south-western France and northern Spain, where more than 100 painted caves have been discovered. Even more cave paintings have been discovered in Australia and southern Africa. Artists usually painted animals from the side, using natural colors, such as black, chestnut-brown, yellow ochre, and red. Paint was made from crushed rocks and other natural substances which stuck to the damp cave walls. Sometimes water and animal or vegetable oils were mixed in to form a paste. Color was applied with fingers, with brushes of feathers, fur, moss, or sticks, or blown from a bone tube. Stones were used as palettes with large shells as containers. This large outlined bull is made up of patterns and shading using dabs of paint and thick and thin black lines. Layers of smaller animals cross its path.

Words that appear in the text in bold, **like this**, are explained in the glossary on page 31.

CONTENTS

WHAT WAS PREHISTORIC ART?

Put simply, prehistoric people were people who did not have writing. Different groups of people left the prehistoric period at different times, when they started to use writing. Prehistoric art is art made during this period. Some people still have no writing. They live today as their **ancestors** did. The art they make today is still called prehistoric art.

The development of writing was different all over the world. The earliest writing we know about was invented in Sumeria around 3250 B.C. This first writing was little pictures, or **pictograms**, not alphabets like the one we use. Soon people began using **stylized** picture symbols to write about themselves and what they did. Today, these pictures help us understand early peoples.

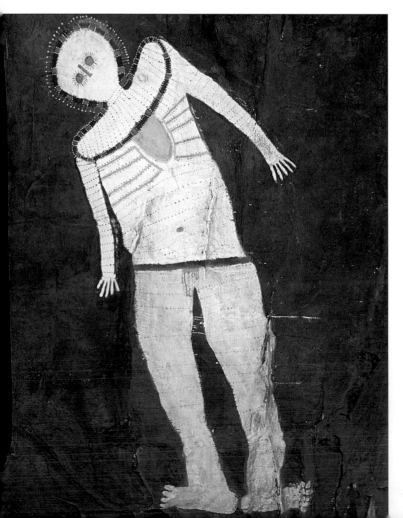

Wandjina Rain Spirit, Kimberley in Western Australia, rock painting.

Australian Aborigines are made up of over 750 tribal groups. White Wandjina spirits like this were painted thousands of years ago on rock surfaces, in the Kimberley region of Western Australia. The Wandjina spirits are very powerful spirit-beings recognized by some Aboriginal groups of this region as being responsible for storms and rain. Clouds encircle the spirit's head like a halo.

*Stonehenge in England, about 2000 B.C., **Neolithic**, 18 ft high, stone.*

*This is one of the most striking ancient monuments still standing. Huge pieces of stone were cut and placed upright in a circle, with others laid on top of them. It was made by European Neolithic people, and is known as a **megalith**. Megaliths were used as tombs or for religious purposes.*

TIMECHART

The first art

There have been humans on Earth for more than four million years. But we have no record of art before about 35,000 years ago. We don't know much about the first artists, but we can find clues in the art itself. Most art seems to have been made for special purposes or was to do with certain beliefs.

BC	EUROPE	MIDDLE EAST	AFRICA	ASIA	THE AMERICAS	AUSTRALASIA
35,000	Paleolithic period					Rock art
25,000	Venus statues					
15,000	Relief sculpture				Cave art —Brazil	
	E N D O F I C E A G E					
10,000	Mesolithic period					
8000	Neolithic period		Rock art —Sahara	Pottery —China		
4000	Rock paintings and pottery					Aborigine bark paintings and carvings
3500		Sumerians and Egyptians develop writing —pictograms				
2000	Megaliths Mycenean civilization —Greece		Sahara begins to dry out		Olmec sculpture	
1000		Iron first used	Nok carvings			
AD						
150						Polynesian tribal art
700						Maori art in New Zealand
800					Tribal art— sand painting, totem art	
1000			Ife Kingdom sculptures			

IDEAS AND MEANINGS

Because prehistoric people had no writing, they did not leave us records about what they thought or did. So, to find out about their thoughts on art, we have to look for evidence in the art itself.

Magic art

One of the first and most important reasons why people created images seems to be because they believed art was a form of magic. They believed art could protect them against other powers, like the forces of nature or unearthly gods. Some art was made to ask the spirits for success in hunting or for the birth of babies.

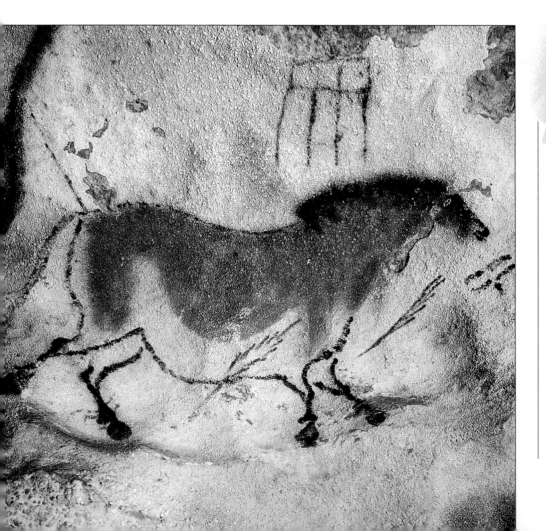

*Galloping Horse, Lascaux in France, about 13,000 B.C., **Paleolithic**, 4½ ft, cave painting.*

This was painted on the walls of an underground cave. Many similar paintings have been discovered in caves in other parts of France and in Spain. Some people believe these paintings were made to help hunters catch their prey in a magical way.

Clues and evidence

Artists took a lot of trouble to make these pictures. Several clues help solve the mystery of why they were painted. Many are of hunting scenes. Sometimes an animal's insides, like the heart, are drawn outside the animal. Maybe this was to show which parts the hunter should aim to hit.

More importantly, pictures were often painted on top of each other. Some are almost completely covered up by other paintings. This may show that the paintings were meant to be more than just beautiful pictures.

Perhaps if some wall paintings were thought to have made a hunt successful, then that piece of wall may have been seen as lucky. People would then have wanted to use the same piece of wall again for more paintings.

Many footprints have been found on the hard, clay floor in front of the pictures. It is possible people danced there, in a kind of ceremony. Similar clues about prehistoric art have been discovered in other parts of the world.

*Horseman of the Altai, Pazyryk in Siberia, about 400 B.C., **Neolithic**, felt.*

This felt wall hanging was made by arctic people in Siberia. It was preserved by the frozen surroundings. It shows how riders dressed, the weapons they carried, the fashion for fancy mustaches, and how skillful the artists were.

MATERIALS AND METHODS

Prehistoric artists probably spent years learning and practicing their craft. Many sketches and corrected drawings have been found alongside other surviving prehistoric pictures. This may be evidence that skilled older artists taught younger ones.

Hand prints

Some of the earliest images that have been found were made by families. They are hand prints. Adults and children placed their hands against a greased wall and blew **pigment** through hollow sticks over them. When they took their hands away, the hand shape was left.

Finger painting

Early artists created skillful and realistic images. Pictures of animals found in caves were produced using the most basic tools and equipment. We think that artists applied paint by blowing through hollow sticks or bones. They also used leather pads, feathers, fur, sticks with the ends crunched (or chewed) into a kind of brush, or their fingers.

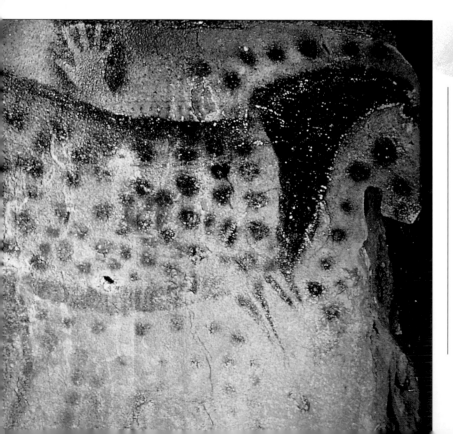

*Hand prints, Pêch-Merle in France, about 18,000 B.C., **Paleolithic**, cave print.*

Can you see the hand prints above the spotted horses? Hands were used as stencils, pressed against the rock and color was blown over them. Color-stained bone tubes have been found that held the powder. Hands were powerful symbols in prehistoric times. They could use tools and utensils. They could also make things and signal to other people.

The Great Serpent Mound, Ohio, 100 B.C.— 500 A.D., approximately 492 yds long, earthwork.

Some works of art were not made with paint at all. This huge snake-like mound was built by the Adena people. It is thought to be a religious monument, because it can only be seen clearly from above. Imagining the artists heaping soil into the serpent shape. Other animal-shaped mounds were made in the same way.

How paints were made

Paints were made by crushing **minerals** into powder and putting them onto damp surfaces, like rock. Sometimes the powder was mixed with wax or oil to make it stick to other surfaces, such as hide, wood, or bone. Powdered pigments were kept in hollow, bone tubes.

Crushed rocks and soil produced browns, yellows, reds, and oranges. Powdered **charcoal** gave black. Another rock, called manganese, produced violet. Chalk made white. Greens and blues came from crushed rocks, but these rocks were not found everywhere in the world.

THE FIRST ARTISTS

The oldest art we know about was made by the people of the **Paleolithic** or Old Stone Age period (from about 35,000 B.C. to 10,000 B.C.). This was during the last Ice Age, which lasted for thousands of years, and was actually several alternating cold and warm periods. The art includes cave paintings, hand prints, and small statues.

Lifelike pictures

Paleolithic cave paintings were first discovered in France and Spain. Similar paintings have since been found in other parts of the world. At first **archaeologists** did not believe that such skillful pictures could have been created by primitive people. But they changed their minds when stone and bone tools used by the Paleolithic artists were found nearby.

The Hall of Bulls, Lascaux in France, about 12,000 B.C., Paleolithic, largest bull is 18 ft in length, cave painting.

*Paintings of bulls cover the walls and roof of this cave. Most of them were painted showing a side view and are larger than life-size. They were painted carefully so each bull is in **proportion**. They seem to stampede over the walls. Smaller outlines of deer running are in between.*

Make your own cave painting

Materials:
sheet of poster board
paper
paste
gray paint
colored chalk
twigs.

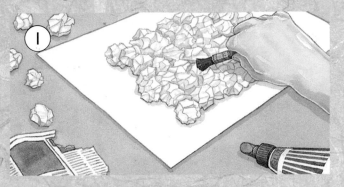

1. Tear paper into small pieces and scrunch it up. Paste it to the poster board and cover it with more paste.

2. Paste on a top layer of torn, but smooth, paper. When this is dry, paint it with gray paint.

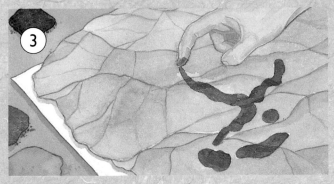

3. When this is dry, crush the chalk and use twigs or your fingers to paint a picture.

Hunting pictures

Paleolithic artists painted the animals they hunted, such as bulls, bison, or mammoths. Many experts think that the artists believed they captured the animal's soul when they painted it. This could be why the images are so lifelike. If the artists captured the animal's true likeness, they thought they would be sure to capture the real thing during the hunt. Whatever the paintings meant, surely no one would have crawled so deep into these caves to paint, unless the pictures had a serious meaning. Dark and eerie, the caves were probably sacred places for Paleolithic people, and the art was part of their beliefs.

THE POWER OF PAINTING

The earliest people spent most of their lives hunting animals and gathering wild fruits. Getting enough food to eat could be a problem. Artists were probably considered to have special powers and perhaps their art was thought to help make hunting successful.

Magical cave paintings

These paintings of animals were made deep inside caves in France, Spain, Africa, North America, and Australia. The caves were far away from where people lived. Artists and tribes seemed to believe that they gained magical powers over animals by painting them.

Some paintings had arrows and spears painted on them or were actually shot at with real weapons after the painting was finished. Perhaps they thought this would help the hunters catch their prey. By painting more animals, maybe they thought they could increase the size of the herds.

Most of the paintings are as large as, or larger than, life. They must have seemed powerful and frightening on the rough walls.

*Jumping Bull and Horses, Lascaux in France, about 16,000 B.C., **Paleolithic**, length 18 ft, cave painting.*

*This large bull is jumping over a **frieze** of little horses. Notice how **shading** helps to make the bull seem lifelike, solid, and strong.*

Evil spirits

Many objects and paintings used for different types of magic have been found around the world. They come from different prehistoric societies. Some of this art was used to cure illnesses or to ward off evil spirits.

How artists worked in the dark

To paint pictures in dark caves, artists made lamps from large hollow stones, seashells, or bowls made from skulls. They filled them with animal fat, then added locks of hair, fur, or pieces of dried moss for wicks and set them on fire.

The "Dead Man," Lascaux in France, about 16,000 B.C., Paleolithic, cave painting.

This painting seems to have a powerful meaning. The bird-headed man has been killed by the bison. The bird on the stick is thought to be the man's spirit. The bison has been killed by a giant spear, but a rhinoceros is escaping unhurt. It seems unlikely that cave paintings like this were for decoration, because many pictures were painted on others. Maybe once a picture had served its special purpose, it was believed to lose its magical powers.

PEOPLE IN PICTURES

Since the first hand prints on cave walls in about 18,000 B.C., people have wanted to produce images of themselves. The earliest artists painted stick figures alongside realistic looking wild animals. Perhaps the human figures were unrealistic because they believed that accurate images stole a person's or animal's soul and they were afraid of taking a person's soul.

A change of art

About 10,000 years ago a warmer climate caused huge forests to cover some of the plains where people had hunted. The warmer climate meant that larger animals could not survive. It seems that at the same time cave art was no longer needed. People moved to areas where they could farm and breed animals. Their life styles were more settled, and they had extra time to create art. Art seems to have been used more for decoration than before. **Mesolithic** (Middle Stone Age) and **Neolithic** (New Stone Age) artists began painting outside on rock surfaces instead of in dark caves. They included more people in their pictures.

Battle Scene, Valltorta in Spain, about 9000 B.C., Mesolithic, length 9½ ft, rock painting.

These lively little Mesolithic figures are **stylized** and very different from the earlier realistic-looking **Paleolithic** cave animals. Painted on rock walls, they form a pattern of curves and angles. **Composition**, or layout, was something new that artists were beginning to consider.

People from Jabbaren, Algeria in Africa, between 6000–1000 B.C., Mesolithic, cave painting.

These people are painted simply, with only one **pigment**. Yet you can see clearly that they are African tribespeople, possibly from one family. Several paintings from this area show us that what is now desert was once fertile farmland.

Caricatures

As you can see from the battle scene, some figures from this period look quite frightening even though they do not look realistic. Some parts of their bodies are exaggerated and some parts are made small. They are **caricatures** of humans.

Prehistoric artists from different societies created caricatures when making human images. Ancient tribes from Papua New Guinea made face masks by painting simple, **geometric** shapes in the right places. They painted a triangle for the nose, circles for the eyes, and so on. Native Americans carved faces on top of each other on totem poles, sometimes including just one or two recognizable features.

PREHISTORIC POTTERY

Prehistoric people used pots to store things and to eat from. At first they made them out of all sorts of materials, including tree bark, leather, bone, and stone. Then about 10,000 years ago, people started to make pottery.

Making pots

First, the clay had to be dug from the ground. It had to be mixed with something dry, like sand, shells, or powdered plants, to make it firm. Then it was rolled and kneaded to make it soft enough to shape. Small containers were easy to make from one piece of clay. Larger pots were often built up with several strips or coils.

Artists discovered that clay hardened and became stronger when it was heated. After each pot had been heated in a fire or oven (fired), it was taken out and smoothed one last time to make sure there were no holes. Many early pots were **engraved** as well as painted. Once the pots had been fired, they could be used to eat or drink from, or to store material, such as grain. Clay pots were particularly important before metals were discovered.

*Urn of Garisu, Kansu in China, about 2500 B.C., **Neolithic**, clay.*

*This jar has been made with one of the earliest **potter's wheels**. By using the wheel, the surface was made smooth and even. The patterns would have been painted on the pot before the clay had dried.*

Beaker people

Although prehistoric tools were simple, the craftwork produced was beautiful. The Beaker people are named after the beaker-like pots that have been found in early Bronze Age graves in Europe. This attractive pottery was made without the help of a potter's wheel. They had delicate patterns stamped on them, in the same way as we print patterns today.

Decorated vessel, Bulgaria in Europe, 6000–5800 B.C., Neolithic, clay.

The people who made vessels like these lived in wooden framed houses in villages in Bulgaria. They often shaped their pots like animals. The surface patterns were popular in the area at that time.

RELIEF CARVING

Relief carving is a mix of drawing and sculpture. Relief pictures are raised from the surface. To make them artists have to be able to draw, carve, and use different tools. Prehistoric relief pictures were made in rock, stone, bone, horn, and wood.

Carved caves

In southern France and Spain in about 19,000 B.C., rock faces were carved with **friezes** of animals (cows, bison, ibex, deer, birds, and even badgers).

Artists used the natural lumps and bumps of the rock surfaces to create animals' shoulders or backs. In the flickering light of prehistoric lamps these carved animal pictures must have appeared to move around the shadowy caves. Other similar cave carvings have been found elsewhere in Europe, often in the darkest depths. Later carvings have been found on open-air rock surfaces or in shallow caves in Eastern Europe.

Stags and Salmon Engraving, Lortet in France, 15,000–8000 B.C., **Paleolithic**, *stone.*

This **engraving** *shows a stag looking backwards. This is an unusual and difficult angle and a change from the flat, sideways-on view that most paintings showed. You can also see how artists were making marks to show light and shade and fur and scales.*

Bison Spear-thrower, Dordogne in France, about 12,000 B.C., Paleolithic, reindeer antler.

This carving on a reindeer antler was found in a cave called La Madeleine in the south of France. It was used for holding and throwing spears. It is quite lifelike and has turned its head to lick its side.

From carving to engraving

Most relief carving was done between 21,000 and 12,000 B.C. After then, engraving was used more often. Engraving means carving inwardly, rather than making raised images. As engraving became more common, so too did **stylized** patterns and pictures. Carving became less lifelike and more **geometric**.

Good luck charms

Bones and antlers were carved with pictures of animals, such as bison, mammoths, wild horses, or deer. Some show humans following the animals. These carvings may have been used as good luck charms and carried on hunting trips.

STATUES AND SCULPTURE

Some of the most mysterious pieces of prehistoric art are plump, little female statues with no faces. They have been named Venus figurines. More than 60 Venus figurines have been found throughout Europe, from Spain to Russia. They date from around 25,000 to 15,000 B.C.

The Bronze Age

Prehistoric sculptors became highly skilled in using all kinds of local materials. These depended on where they lived, but included stone, bone, shell, horn, bark, or wood. Many also modeled in clay. When metals were discovered in about 4000 B.C. many sculptors worked in copper and **bronze**. Bronze was easier to work with than stone and better than any other material then known. Its use spread across the world, giving its name to the Bronze Age.

*Venus Figurine, Willendorf in Austria, about 25,000 B.C., **Paleolithic**, 5 in., limestone.*

This is the best known of the Venus figurines. She was once painted red. Some traces of the paint remain. Perhaps people believed that these plump or pregnant women were mother-goddesses and could help women have babies.

Wrong proportions

Some **terracotta** heads were found in Africa. They were made in about 300 B.C. They are the same size as real heads, with detailed eyes, noses, mouths, and complicated hairstyles. Some were attached to much smaller bodies. We do not know exactly what they were for or why they were out of **proportion** to their bodies. But we do know that they were believed to please the spirits.

Guardian Figures, Easter Island, about 1000 A.D., **Mesolithic***, 13–16 ft high, rock.*

These enormous human-like statues guard Easter Island in the Pacific. The eyes are made of white coral. Tattoos are painted on the bodies. Nobody today knows why they were made or who made them. They do not appear to represent real people, but they are human-shaped. They seem to guard the island, or perhaps they are looking out to sea for something.

PACIFIC ART

Many different groups of people lived around the Pacific Ocean, from the Aborigines in Australia to the Polynesians. The Polynesians spread south to New Zealand, from Hawaii in the north and Easter Island in the east. Most early islanders lived in tribes, hunting, farming, and fishing. Most Pacific tribes honored the spirits of their **ancestors**, believing that they had the power to bring good or bad luck. The Pacific peoples had different styles and different ideas of beauty. Some Pacific art was realistic and some was **stylized**.

Aboriginal art

For thousands of years the art of the Australian Aborigines has been an important part of their lives. It includes bark and rock paintings, rock carvings, shell **engravings**, and wooden sculptures. Aborigines decorated many of the objects they used in everyday life, such as spears, boomerangs, and baskets. Today they believe that art should not be locked up in museums.

Kangaroo Dreaming, Australia 1989, synthetic polymer on canvas.

Dreamings relate to creation times in the Aboriginal religious tradition. This picture talks about the creative activity of one of the great creature-beings who took the form of a kangaroo. This painting describes a section of the kangaroo's journey through one group's land.

Amazing skills

Many Pacific artists developed amazing skills. Considering the simple tools they used, much of their detailed work was astonishing. In New Zealand, Maori woodcarving is extremely complicated and is still made today. As well as being complicated or detailed, much of this art also shows great freedom of imagination and expression. Each tribe had their own style, but individual artists had their own interpretations. Artists knew that they were producing art that was meant to last, even when it was made for a single festive occasion.

Maori Carved Head, Waitangi in New Zealand, about 800 A.D., woodcarving with inlaid shell eyes.

This head represents a Maori ancestor who would have been recognized by his distinctive pattern of facial tattoos. To the Maori, facial tattoos were a sign of great courage and revealed a person's true personality.

AFRICAN ART

Africa stretches across nearly 12 million square miles. It is said to be the birthplace of the human race, and some of the earliest art has been found there. There were many different tribes in Africa, who did not know that others existed. The first works of art produced there were paintings and **engravings** in the Sahara before it was a desert, in about 7000 B.C. Pictures have been found on rock surfaces that seem to be about ancient tribal beliefs.

Tribal traditions

Artists were probably given work to do by chieftains, heads of families, and other important people. In some tribes the job of artist was often passed from father to son. Training probably lasted for many years. Artists had to learn the traditions of both the art and religion of their tribe. Some tribal art involved music and dancing as well as decorative carvings, statues, and masks.

*Herdsman and Cattle, Tassili in Algeria, about 6500 B.C., **Mesolithic**, the figures are between 3–12 ft high, rock painting.*

This rock painting of copper-colored farmers, comes from the Sahara region of Africa. It shows us that the Sahara was once fertile and how the people farmed. All the mountainous regions of the Sahara contain rock paintings.

Art for the spirits

Like the art of the Pacific regions, it seems that much African art was made to please the spirits. The art of different tribes shows that they believed in different spirits and traditions.

Some of the finest African art was sculpture. This included masks and statues made from wood, ivory, stone, **terracotta**, raffia, mud and, later, iron, and **bronze**. Artists carved statuettes that were probably thought to have healing and protecting powers.

*Bronze figure, Ife in West Africa, about 1200 A.D., **Paleolithic**, 15 ft, bronze.*

*This statue may be of a king. Advanced **techniques** (the process was later lost) have been used to make it. Perhaps these skilled artists learned their techniques from other more advanced tribes who moved in to the area. Similar terracotta sculptures were found less than 18 miles away. They were possibly made by other tribes, but we do not know for sure.*

AMERICAN ART

As in Africa, American tribes grew up far away from each other. Each tribe developed its own beliefs and colorful art. About 32,000 years ago, stone age hunters arrived in North America and traveled south into what is now Mexico.

Gradually different civilizations developed. The Olmecs in southern Mexico, for example, developed building methods and designed picture-signs which are only now just beginning to be understood. They carved huge stone heads, some more than ten feet high. These are probably **portraits** of their most important people.

*Olmec Colossal Head, Mexico, from about 1500 to 300 B.C., **Mesolithic** to **Neolithic**, 8–11 ft, stone.*

This stone head is one of sixteen that is believed to have been made by the Olmec civilization.
They each weigh about 10 tons. We are not sure if they are the heads of gods or rulers, but they all have similar faces and wear circular helmets.

North America

Some of the hunters who came from Asia into North America spread across the United States and Canada and formed many different tribal groups.

Native American peoples, like the Inuits from the arctic regions, the Sioux from the great plains, and the various pueblo-dwellers of the southwest, are the descendants of these early stone age hunters.

The early North Americans left behind objects that we use today to identify the different tribes, such as pottery, tools, animal-shaped mounds, sculptures, and sand pictures.

South America

Groups of peoples also spread throughout Central and South Amerca. The earliest civilization in South America seems to have been the Chavin, who lived in the Andes Mountains from about 1250 B.C. to 200 B.C. They made pottery, tools, weapons, sculptures, and carvings.

There are many other early Central and South American tribal groups, each with their own types of art. We can identify where different groups lived by examining the types of art they left behind.

Copper Bird, Ohio, about 100 B.C., **Neolithic***, 15 in., copper and pearl.*

This bird, which is a raven or a crow, was made by an artist from the Ohio River valley. Several more sculptures of animals have been found nearby. Although the artist used few materials and worked with simple tools, the bird is quite detailed.

UNDERSTANDING PREHISTORIC ART

Inventive art

Prehistoric art shows us clearly how art changes as people's life styles change. It also shows that the most realistic art is not necessarily the most skillful. Sometimes the ideas and imagination behind the art are more important than the technical skills. The first prehistoric artists had to depend more on their natural skills than later artists who developed better tools and equipment. This shows us how inventive artists can be.

How styles developed

By the end of the **Paleolithic** period, artists had developed three styles. Art has changed since then. But even now, it usually follows one of these first three styles.

1. Natural art

(a realistic-looking, recognizable copy of something).

Jade figure, Mexico, about 400 B.C., **Neolithic**, jade.

Although the Olmec people (about 1250 to 400 B.C.) had only Stone Age tools, they were gifted sculptors. This statue is made of a semi-precious, green stone called jade and is probably a likeness of one of their kings or gods. We do not know who he was, but we can see it is an accurate and recognizable description of a man.

2. Picture signs

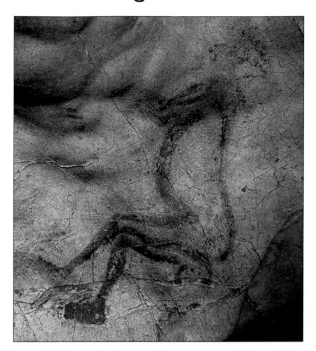

Sorcerer, Trois Frères in France,
about 15,000 B.C., **Paleolithic**,
30 in. high, cave painting.

This painting, known as the Sorcerer,
was found on the wall of a cave in
France. It shows a man with antlers on
his head who may have been taking
part in a **ritual** dance. Perhaps he is
asking the spirits for a successful hunt.
It is not a realistic representation, but
it is a simple picture that could be
understood by others.

3. Decorative patterns

Patterned pot, Romania,
about 4000 B.C., Neolithic,
height 5½ in., clay.

Swirls, spirals, circles, and zigzags
became popular pottery decorations
during the Stone Age. **Archaeologists**
can sometimes tell where a pot was
made by looking at its pattern.
Geometric patterns were used after
lifelike cave art became less important,
and people had more time to create art.

Primitive pictures

Primitive art is different to prehistoric
art. Primitive art is usually based on a
simple view of what the artist knew to
be there. It was not based on a careful
look at an object.

Some prehistoric artists made
primitive art, but they were also
skilled at non-primitive art such as
realistic animal paintings and statues.
Which kind of art do you prefer?

TIME LINE

GLOSSARY

ancestors These are members of the same family, but ones who lived long ago.

archaeologists People who study the past by looking at old remains and objects are called archaeologists.

bronze This is a hard-wearing, brownish-gold metal, a mixture of copper and tin.

caricatures Pictures or imitations of people that exaggerate certain features are called caricatures.

charcoal This is the black material that is left when wood or bones are burned.

composition The layout, or arrangement, of art is called its composition.

engraved/engravings Engraving is carving into something to make a picture or a pattern. The pictures are called engravings.

friezes Bands or strips of decoration are called friezes.

geometric Lines, angles, and shapes, such as squares, triangles and circles are geometric patterns.

Megalith This is a large monument made of stones or boulders.

Mesolithic The time period between about 10,000 B.C. and 8000 B.C. is the Mesolithic Period.

minerals Natural rocks or stones can contain or be made of minerals.

Neolithic The time period between about 8000 B.C. and 5000 B.C. is the Neolithic Period. It is also called the New Stone Age.

Paleolithic The time from when humans first started using stone tools until about 10,000 B.C. It is also called the Old Stone Age.

pictograms These are little pictures used as symbols to mean something.

pigment This is colored powder made from plants, minerals, or animals and mixed with various liquids to make paint.

portrait This is an image of a particular person.

potter's wheel This is a circle of wood or stone that was spun around with wet clay on it, so that the sides of a pot could be pulled up and smoothed easily.

proportion This is when things are the correct size in relation to each other.

relief A raised carved picture is a relief.

rituals These are religious or community ceremonies.

shading Adding deeper color in darker areas is called shading.

stylized A way of designing something that makes it simpler, but also decorative, is known as making it stylized.

techniques These are ways of working.

terracotta This word means "baked earth." It is clay, usually reddish-brown, used to make pottery and statues.

More Books to Read

Corbishley, Mike. *What Do we Know About Prehistoric People?* New York: Peter Bedrick, 1994.

Stone Age People. Chicago: World Book, 1996.

INDEX

Numbers in plain type (24) refer to the text. Numbers in bold type (**28**) refer to an illustration.